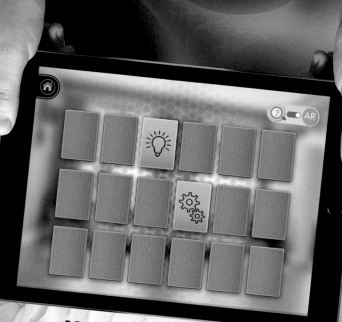

Match the pairs to see how your brain makes MEMORIES!

Use the brain scanner to see YOUR BRAIN!

Take a closer look at the SECTIONS of your brain and what they do!

Get ready to understand how your brain works, and how it makes you YOU!

Executive Editor: Alexandra Koken
Design Manager: Emily Clarke
Design and diagrams: WildPixel Ltd
Cover illustration: WildPixel Ltd
Picture research: Steve Behan
Production: Yael Steinitz

PICTURE CREDITS
The publishers would like to thank the following sources for their kind permission to reproduce
the pictures in this book:
4-5. Billion Photos/Shutterstock.com, 6. Cosmin4000/iStockphoto.com (top), J.Barber/ Custom Medical
Stock Photo/Science Photo Library (centre), Sci-Comm Studios/Science Photo Library (bottom), 7. Rainer
Plendl/Shutterstock.com (top), Philippe Psaila/Science Photo Library (centre), PR Michel Zanca/ISM/
Science Photo Library (centre right), 8. Arthur Glauberman/Science Photo Library (top), CNRI/Science
Photo Library (centre), 8-9. Leigh Prather/Shutterstock.com, 9. Nancy Kedersha/Science Photo Library,
10-11. Yodiyim/Shutterstock.com, 11. Syda Productions/Shutterstock.com (top), A.Katz/Shutterstock.
com (bottom), 12. Alexandre Zveiger/Shutterstock.com (centre), Firstsignal/iStockphoto.com (inset
top), Decade4d/Anatomy Online/Shutterstock.com (inset centre), Alliance/Shutterstock.com (bottom),
13. Billion Photos/Shutterstock.com (top left), AGrigorjeva/iStockphoto.com (top right), Decade4d/
Anatomy Online/Shutterstock.com (bottom), 16. Springer MEdizin/Science Photo Library (centre), Steve
Gschmeissner/Science Photo Library (bottom), 17. Objowl/Shutterstock.com (top), University Tubingen/
DPA/PA Images (bottom), 18-19. Fotos593/Shutterstock.com, 19. Microscape/Science Photo Library (top),
Martyn F. Chillmaid/Science Photo Library (bottom), 20. Ollyy/Shutterstock.com, 21. ESB Professional/
Shutterstock.com (top left), Syda Productions/Shutterstock.com (top right), Rawpixel.com/Shutterstock.
com (centre), Gelpi/Shutterstock.com (bottom), 22. Aneta Jungerova/Shutterstock.com, 22-23.
Sciencepix/Shutterstock.com, 23. Johanna Goodyear/Shutterstok.com (top), LDprod/Shutterstock.com
(bottom), 24. Living Art Enterprises/Science Photo Library, 25. Shutterstock.com (top), Dmitry Naumov/
Shutterstock.com (centre), Patrick Landmann/Science Photo Library (bottom), 27. Littlekidmoment/
Science Photo Library (top), Shelia Terry/Science Photo Library (centre), Wunkley/Alamy Stock Photo
(bottom), 28. Don Arnold, University of Southern California, 28-29. Shutterstock.com, 29. Pressmaster/
Shutterstock.com, Denver Post Photo by Cyrus McCrimmon (bottom), 30-31. Christopher Bird/PA Archive/
PA Images, 31. Chai Seamaker/Shutterstock.com (top), Digital Storm/Shutterstock.com (centre)

Every effort has been made to acknowledge correctly and contact the source and/or copyright holder of
each picture and Carlton Books Limited apologises for any unintentional errors or omissions that will be
corrected in future editions of this book.

Need some help? Check out our useful website for
helpful tips and problem-solving advice:
www.carltonbooks.co.uk/digital-magic-help

THE BRAIN

VENTURE INSIDE YOUR HEAD WITH AUGMENTED REALITY

JACK CHALLONER

CARLTON
KIDS

WHAT'S INSIDE YOUR HEAD?

Your brain allows you to sense the world, to move your body, to remember things and to feel happy or sad. It keeps you alive by making your heart beat and your lungs fill with air, and to feel hungry. It allows you to think about things, and to read, write, speak and listen. So just what is this amazing thing inside your head?

Parietal lobe

Frontal lobe

Occipital lobe

Cerebellum

Spinal cord

Medulla oblongata

Pons

WELCOME TO YOUR BRAIN

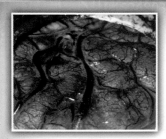

In this photograph taken during brain surgery, you can see the brain's folded outer surface, the cerebrum.

A living brain has the same consistency as a piece of uncooked meat: soft and squishy. It has a mass of about 1.3 kilograms, about the same as a medium-sized melon, and it's about the same size and shape as two fists held together. It is covered in three membranes, called meninges. The first two are thin and clear, and between them is a fluid that helps nourish the brain and support it. The outer membrane is thick and strong. Above that is the skull and a layer of skin called the scalp.

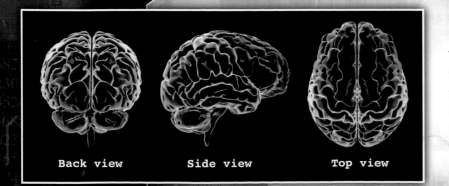

Back view   Side view   Top view

THE CEREBRUM

The first thing you see when you look at a brain is the cerebrum: the wrinkled part that looks a bit like a walnut. It is involved in many of the things we normally think of the brain as doing: thinking, remembering, sensing the world and making our bodies move. If you could unfold the cerebrum, and straighten out its wrinkles, it would be about the size of a tea towel. The cerebrum is divided into two halves, or hemispheres, and brain scientists divide each hemisphere into 'lobes'.

UNDERNEATH THE CEREBRUM

At the back and below the cerebrum is the cerebellum (the name means 'little brain'). Also hidden underneath the cerebrum are the parts of the brain involved in emotions and memory. Below them is the brainstem, which is involved in unconscious actions, such as keeping your heart beating. The brainstem leads to the spinal cord, which connects the brain to the rest of the body.

BRAIN UNDER PRESSURE

Your brain works hard day and night, making sure your body functions properly, but it works hardest of all when you have a problem to solve. When you are struggling over a very difficult question, or trying to figure out what to do in a complicated situation, your brain calls on its powers of memory, emotion, logical reasoning, planning and prediction.

FUN FACT!

The brain makes up about 2% of the body's weight but uses about 20% of the body's energy supply.

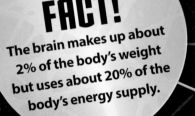

When a part of the brain needs to work harder, blood flow to that part increases to give it more energy. An MRI scanner produces very strong magnetic fields, which can detect a chemical in the blood called haemoglobin. The greater the blood flow, the more haemoglobin is present and the more the magnetic field is affected. This is how scientists can watch which part of the brain is working hardest.

THE BRAIN ACTIVATION PAGE

Scan your brain with Augmented Reality!

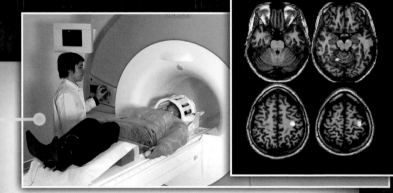

WATCHING THE BRAIN AT WORK

All of your brain is working all the time, but different parts specialize in particular jobs. There are specific areas of the cerebrum that process information from the eyes, while other areas are involved in producing speech. Similarly, there are parts of the brain beneath the cerebrum that select and process memories for storage. Neuroscientists (people who study the brain) can find out which parts are involved in which jobs by using an MRI scanner, 'MRI' stands for 'magnetic resonance imaging'.

7

USE YOUR BRAIN CELLS

Your body is made up of lots of different types of cell. For example, there are skin cells, muscle cells, and cells in your stomach that produce acid to help digest your food. Your brain contains two main types of cell: neurons and glial cells. The neurons do the business of thinking, remembering and sensing the world, and the glial cells nourish and support the neurons. Unlike most cells, which are tiny and round, neurons can be very long, with branching strands called axons and dendrites extending from the centre of the cell.

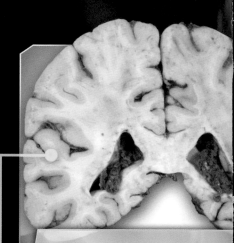

Brains can be kept for years and studied — but to stop them rotting they are stored in a liquid called a fixative. Most of the blood is removed from the brain, making it lighter in colour.

A TANGLE OF WIRES

Inside your brain there are an unimaginably large number of cells: about 100 billion neurons and at least as many glial cells. Each neuron connects to many others – typically around a thousand. So the number of connections in the brain is larger still – more than 100 trillion! These connections become stronger or weaker with experience – that is how we learn and how our memories are stored.

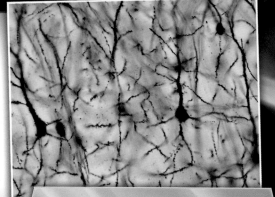

This photograph shows a tiny section of a brain seen under a microscope. Some of the neurons have been coloured dark by a special pigment.

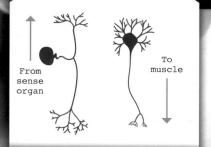

From sense organ

To muscle

Left: sensory neuron, with dendrites at the bottom. Right: motor neuron, dendrites at the top, axon at the bottom, activating a muscle.

TYPES OF NEURON

All neurons have long strands called axons and dendrites. An axon carries a tiny electrical current from one end to the other whenever the neuron 'fires' – this is how information is carried around the brain and body. The dendrites connect to the axons of other cells, and detect whether the other cells are firing. Sensory neurons carry information from cells in sense organs, such as the eyes, while motor neurons activate muscle cells. There are also interneurons, which connect only to other neurons. Axons and dendrites divide into many branches, so they can pass on or detect signals from many other cells.

WHITE AND GREY

A fresh or living brain looks pink, because it is filled with blood. However, some parts look pinkish-white and some look pinkish-grey. When a brain is preserved in a laboratory, these areas instead look white and grey. The 'white matter' is where most of the axons and dendrites of long motor and sensory neurons are found. Grey matter is where most of the cell bodies and glial cells are.

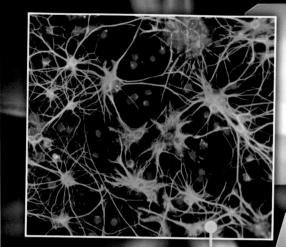

SUPPORT WORKERS

There are lots of different types of glial cell inside your brain. Some help to hold neurons in place and hold them apart; some supply the neurons with nutrients and oxygen; some destroy viruses or bacteria; and some safely dispose of dead neurons.

```
The most common type of glial cell is the
astrocyte. These star-shaped cells make up
about a third of all glial cells. They carry
out a large number of different functions,
including regulating the supply of glucose,
which is the fuel for neurons.
```

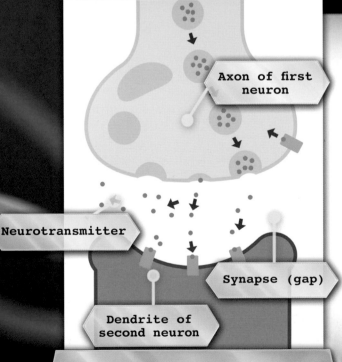

Axon of first neuron

Neurotransmitter

Synapse (gap)

Dendrite of second neuron

```
Neurotransmitters are passed across the gap
between the axon of one neuron and the
dendrite of another. It's amazing that this
is how we think, remember and sense the world.
```

JUMPING THE GAP

Each neuron is a separate cell, but the way the brain works is all about connections, so a thought, a memory or a sensation is a huge number of interconnected neurons firing in a pattern. The connections are called synapses. A synapse is actually a tiny gap – between an axon belonging to one cell and a dendrite belonging to another. When a neuron fires, the electric current passes along the axon, and when it reaches the synapse, it causes the cell to release chemical compounds called neurotransmitters. These compounds pass across the gap and connect with special receptors on the dendrite. The dendrite then creates a signal that passes to the neuron's cell body.

BRAIN-BODY CONNECTIONS

Your brain receives and sends signals to and from your body, so that it can sense the world around you, and make your muscles work to move your body. The signals pass along axons — the long fibres of brain cells (neurons). Those axons are bundled together to form nerves and, running up the middle of your spine, a thicker bundle is called the spinal cord.

CONNECTED SYSTEM

Your brain, spinal cord and nerves together make up your nervous system. The brain and spinal cord form the 'central nervous system', while the collection of nerves reaching out to all parts of the body is called the 'peripheral nervous system'. Most nerves connect to the spinal cord, but the twelve pairs of 'cranial nerves,' which come from your eyes, ears, tongue, nose, facial muscles and chest, connect to the base of the brain.

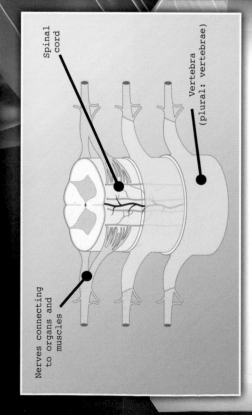

Spinal cord

Vertebra
(plural: vertebrae)

Nerves connecting
to organs and
muscles

SPINAL CORD

Passing down through holes in the bones of your spine (your vertebrae) is a thick bundle of axons called the spinal cord. Signals from the brain to muscles and organs around the body pass down this, and signals from the body pass up to the brain. Just like the brain itself, the spinal cord is surrounded and protected by thick membranes called meninges. Nerves emerge from the spinal cord through holes in the vertebrae.

FUNNY BONE

Have you ever hit your elbow and felt a weird tingling sensation? If so, people probably told you that you had hit your funny bone. It's called that because of the strange sensation you feel afterwards – but, in fact, it's not a bone at all: it's a nerve, called the ulnar nerve, which connects your spinal cord to your hand.

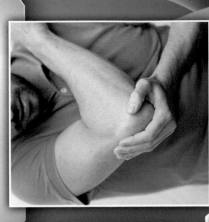

INSIDE A NERVE

A nerve contains tens or hundreds of individual nerve fibres – the axons of neurons. Each individual fibre can only carry signals in one direction: the fibres of sensory neurons carry signals towards the brain, while motor neuron fibres carry signals away from the brain. Most nerves contain only one type of nerve fibre, so they only pass information in one direction – either towards or away from the brain. Those containing sensory nerve fibres are called afferent nerves, while those carrying motor nerve fibres are called efferent nerves.

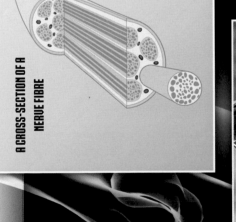

A CROSS-SECTION OF A NERVE FIBRE

BREAKING THE CONNECTION

The spinal cord is a vital connection between the brain and the body. If people have bad accidents and they damage or even break their spinal cord, signals will be unable to pass to and from the brain. As a result they will be paralysed – unable to move their muscles – and will also lose sensation in part of their body. The exact effects of this kind of injury depend upon how far down the spinal cord the damage occurs. Low down, only the nerves supplying the legs will be cut off – but near the top of the spinal cord, the arms and much of the body will also be affected.

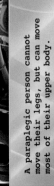

A paraplegic person cannot move their legs, but can move most of their upper body.

YOUR BRAIN IN AUTOMATIC

Many parts of your brain get on with their jobs without you being aware of what they are doing. One of the most important is the brainstem, which is located where the spinal cord meets the base of the brain. The brainstem is responsible for passing signals between the spinal cord and the brain but it also controls your breathing and regulates your heart rate – all without you having to think about it.

Midbrain

Pons

Brainstem

Medulla

UNCONSCIOUS CONTROL

The brainstem is a crucial part of your brain. It is divided into three main sections: the midbrain, the pons and the medulla. All three parts connect the spinal cord and the brain, and they constantly and unconsciously monitor many of your body's vital functions – including breathing, circulation and digestion. The medulla also plays a part in activating the muscle movements that allow swallowing, sneezing, hiccuping and vomiting.

After exercise, your breathing rate typically increases from about fifteen to as many as fifty breaths per minute.

CATCHING YOUR BREATH

When you exercise, your muscles use up oxygen more quickly and produce more carbon dioxide as a waste product. The carbon dioxide dissolves in your blood, making the blood slightly acidic. The brainstem contains neurons that can detect how acidic the blood is. When the acidity rises, the brainstem automatically increases your breathing rate – to draw in more oxygen and to get rid of more carbon dioxide – and your heart rate, to get the oxygen to where it is needed.

It is impossible to sneeze without closing your eyelids, because the parts of the brainstem that make you sneeze automatically make your eyelids close as well!

ATCHOO!

Sneezing is a reflex action, which expels potentially harmful things, such as dust or bacteria, from your nose and airways. It involves many different muscles in the throat and chest all working together. The whole thing is orchestrated in the brainstem.

CONSCIOUSNESS...

The words 'conscious' means 'aware' – so consciousness is simply awareness of yourself and the world around you. The brainstem works without conscious control – which means you don't have to think about what it is doing or even be aware of it: it does it automatically. Weirdly, the brainstem controls your consciousness as well – this makes sense, because you can't consciously keep yourself conscious!

When you are asleep, you are unconscious: your brainstem prevents most information from your senses reaching your brain. It also prevents signals passing the other way, so your brain will no longer be able to send messages to your muscles. The brainstem still monitors your body and even your surroundings, and can wake you if you need to go to the bathroom or there is some kind of danger.

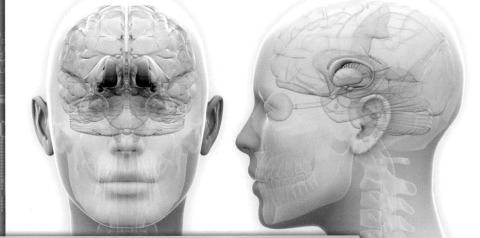

The hypothalamus contains special neurons that act like a thermometer, and it also receives information from temperature-sensing neurons in your skin. When your body's temperature rises, the hypothalamus sends signals to the brainstem and to various parts of the body, which work together to make you sweat.

HYPOTHALAMUS

There is another part of the brain, just above the top of the brainstem, that controls a number of essential, automatic, unconscious actions. For example, the hypothalamus controls hunger and thirst, and even tells the brainstem when to make you go to sleep. One of the hypothalamus's most important functions is regulating your body temperature.

SENSING THE WORLD

One of the most important jobs of your brain is to sense the world around you. Your brain receives signals from receptors, or nerve endings, which are the ends of specialized neurons. There are several kinds of receptor: some detect light, some detect the vibrations of sound waves, some detect hot and cold, some detect pressure. For your senses of taste and smell, there are even receptors that can identify particular substances in food or in the air.

HEAR IT

When a sound wave passes by your head, it makes the air inside your ear canal vibrate. That makes a thin membrane called the eardrum vibrate, too – and these vibrations are passed on, via three little bones, to an organ called the cochlea. The inside of the cochlea is lined with specialized receptor neurons that can detect the vibrations – and those receptors send signals to the brain.

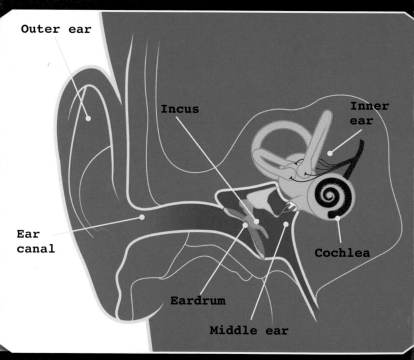

Outer ear

Incus

Inner ear

Ear canal

Cochlea

Eardrum

Middle ear

In your skin there are receptors for heat, pain, touch and pressure. Every hair has a receptor attached to its root, too. Each one sends signals along nerves. Very sensitive areas of the skin, such as your fingertips, have many more receptors than others.

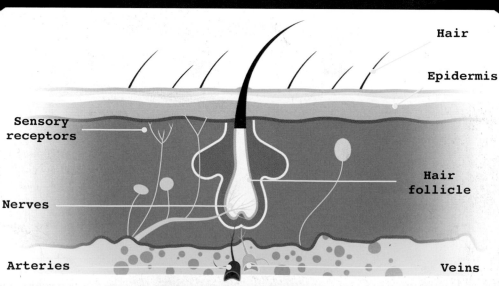

Hair

Epidermis

Sensory receptors

Hair follicle

Nerves

Arteries

Veins

SKIN DEEP

There are several different types of receptor in your skin. They join together into bundles that then join into bigger bundles to form sensory nerves. These nerves then connect to the spinal cord via synapses (see p. 9), and the signals travel up the spinal cord, through the brainstem and into the brain.

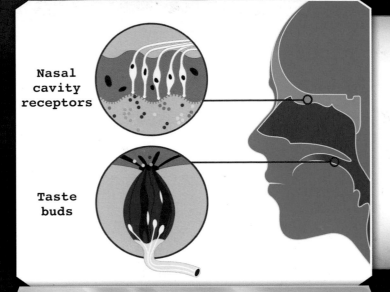

Nasal cavity receptors

Taste buds

In the roof of your nasal cavity are thousands of receptors that can identify particular molecules. Whenever their 'target' molecule hits, they send a signal along nerves to the brain. Receptors in the taste buds of your tongue identify chemical compounds in food in a similar way.

CHEMICAL SENSE

Fruits, flowers, your favourite shampoo – all of these things have chemical compounds that are volatile. That simply means that those compounds lose molecules to the air, by evaporation. The molecules mix with the air, so that when you breathe in through your nose, you also breathe in those molecules. Each smelly thing gives off a particular mixture of compounds, which is why your brain is able to distinguish between different smells.

THE BRAIN
ACTIVATION PAGE

Watch your brain react to sounds!

Hearing

Taste

Visual

Smell

Sensation from skin and organs

PERCEPTION

The signals coming from receptors in your skin, ears, eyes (see pp. 16–17), nose and tongue pass through various parts of the brain, including the area that forms emotions (see pp. 20–21). However, they all end up in the folded outer part of your brain, the cortex, where your brain brings them all together to form a 'perception' of the world around you. Certain areas of the cortex correspond to particular senses, and even to particular parts of the body.

THE SENSE OF SIGHT

Scientists consider the light-sensitive part of each eye – the retina – to be part of the brain. In fact when a baby is growing inside its mother's womb, the neurons of the retina sprout directly from the baby's developing brain. The brain processes information from the retinas, forming a mental picture of the world. And your clever brain can even make you see things that aren't really there...

Lens

Pupil

Cornea

Iris

HOW WE SEE THE WORLD

Light from objects around you enters each eye through a small hole called the pupil and passes through a lens, which focuses the light, just as a camera's lens does. The light forms an image on the retina, which is packed with light-sensitive neurons. Signals from these neurons pass along axons (see p. 8) in optic nerves and end up in various parts of the brain – in particular, an area at the back called the visual cortex.

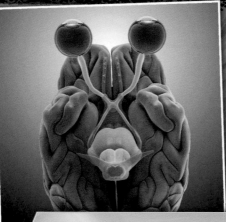

This view of the underside of the brain shows how the two optic nerves meet near the brainstem, in a part of the brain called the optic chiasm. Here, the axons carrying signals from the right half of each retina come together to follow the same path, and neurons from the left half come together and follow a different path. Each set of axons ends up in the back of the cortex, in areas that can make sense of the incoming signals.

CATCHING THE LIGHT

The most important cells in the retina are called rods and cones. When light hits them, these cells absorb the light and produce signals that pass along the cells' axons towards the brain. There are three types of cone: one sensitive to red, one to green and one to blue light. But there is just one kind of rod cell; it can only detect how bright the light is. If you only had rod cells, you would see the world in black and white.

This false-coloured photograph, taken through a microscope, shows rods (the tall, thin beige cells) and cones (the short, green cells) in a human retina.

BLIND SPOT

There is one part of the retina where all the axons of the rod and cone cells gather together to form the optic nerve – a bit like the plughole of a sink. That part of the retina is called the blind spot, because there are no light-sensitive cells there at all. We are not usually aware of a 'hole' in our vision, because the brain fills it in with information from the other eye.

To experience your own blind spot, close your left eye and use your right eye to look at the cross above. Hold the book about 10 cm from your face and move it slowly backwards and forwards until the dot disappears, watching the cross all the time. Now do the same with your right eye closed and your left eye looking at the dot.

Retina

Optic nerve

Blind spot

This picture isn't really moving, but it may look like it is.

NOW YOU SEE IT

The brain plays a very active role in how we see the world. It doesn't just see the image that falls on the retina; it processes the information it receives, and forms a mental picture, which can include colours, edges and even movement that isn't really there.

BLINDNESS

Some people have very limited sense of sight, or no sense of sight at all. People who are blind use their other senses – particularly the sense of touch – to create a mental picture of the world around them. Amazingly, the visual cortex in the brain processes the signals from these senses.

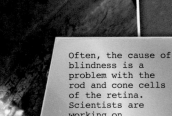

Often, the cause of blindness is a problem with the rod and cone cells of the retina. Scientists are working on electronic sensors that can detect light and send signals to the brain through wires instead of axons. You can see one of these retinal implants in this X-ray photograph.

THE BRAIN
ACTIVATION PAGE

Invert your world with Augmented Reality!

MAKING MOVEMENTS

Your brain directly controls almost every movement your body makes – from lifting your little finger to jumping up and down. Some of the movements you make consciously, on purpose; these are called 'voluntary' movements. Others, like breathing, are directed by your brain but without your having to think about it; these are 'involuntary'. Some involuntary movements are reflexes: very quick responses to things happening – and they could just save your life.

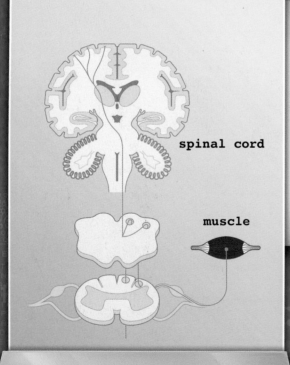

spinal cord

muscle

The neurons in the motor cortex send signals along axons (see p. 8) that reach all the way down the spinal cord. The axons from each side, or hemisphere, of the brain cross over at the bottom of the brainstem — so the right motor cortex controls the muscles in the left side of the body, and vice versa. Nerves connecting to the spinal cord pick up the signals and pass them on to the muscles.

BRAIN IN CONTROL

To make one of your muscles move, your brain sends signals along efferent neurons (see p. 11), down through your spinal cord and out to whichever muscle needs to move. Most of the signals for voluntary movements come from an area of the wrinkled outer part of the brain (the cortex) called the motor cortex.

THE LITTLE BRAIN

One part of the brain, called the cerebellum, is particularly important in making very precise movements that involve several different muscles working at the same time. It controls movements called fine motor skills, which include writing, using scissors and picking up small, delicate things – and it also controls larger skills, such as balancing, walking and standing up straight.

MAKING MUSCLES WORK

Every muscle in your body can only do two things: pull and relax. Most muscles are therefore in pairs: one pulls one way and the other pulls the other. In order to pull, a muscle contracts (shrinks) – and it only does that when signals come along a nerve from the brain.

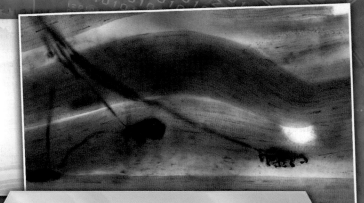

This photograph, taken through a microscope, shows nerve endings in muscle tissue. When a signal reaches the nerve ending, the neuron releases a chemical compound into the gap between nerve and muscle. This sets off a series of chemical reactions inside the muscle cells that make the muscle contract.

The cerebellum receives inputs from all your senses, and it puts all this information together and produces coordinated outputs to muscles that help the whole body move in just the right way, like balancing on a tightrope.

FLOATING ARMS

Try the floating-arm trick and fool your brain into sending signals to make your muscles work. Stand in a doorway and push hard against the frame on both sides as shown. Keep pushing for at least half a minute – longer if possible. Now step away from the doorway and stand still. Your arms should slowly rise, as if they are being lifted by a mysterious force.

THE BRAIN
ACTIVATION PAGE

Watch your brain in action as you test your fine motor skills!

REFLEXES

A reflex is a rapid, involuntary movement your body makes in response to something happening. For example, when an object is hurtling towards you, your brain makes your eyes blink and your body get out of the way.

If you touch something very hot, like a candle flame, a signal rushes along sensory nerve fibres to a small interneuron in your spinal cord. That interneuron triggers motor nerves to activate muscles that pull your arm away. Your brain only becomes aware of what your arm has done after it has moved.

HAPPY BRAIN, SAD BRAIN

You are an emotional person. Sometimes you feel happy or sad; sometimes you are scared, angry or you feel excited. All of these feelings are the result of activity inside your brain, mostly inside a collection of structures underneath the cerebrum, called the limbic system. A number of chemical compounds, called neurotransmitters and hormones, are also involved in creating your mood. Both of these types of compound can affect the way neurons in your brain communicate with each other.

LIMBIC SYSTEM

The components of the limbic system receive inputs from all your senses, as well as the 'thinking' part of the brain, the frontal cortex. They are mostly responsible for producing your brain's emotional responses – everything from total joy to outright disgust!

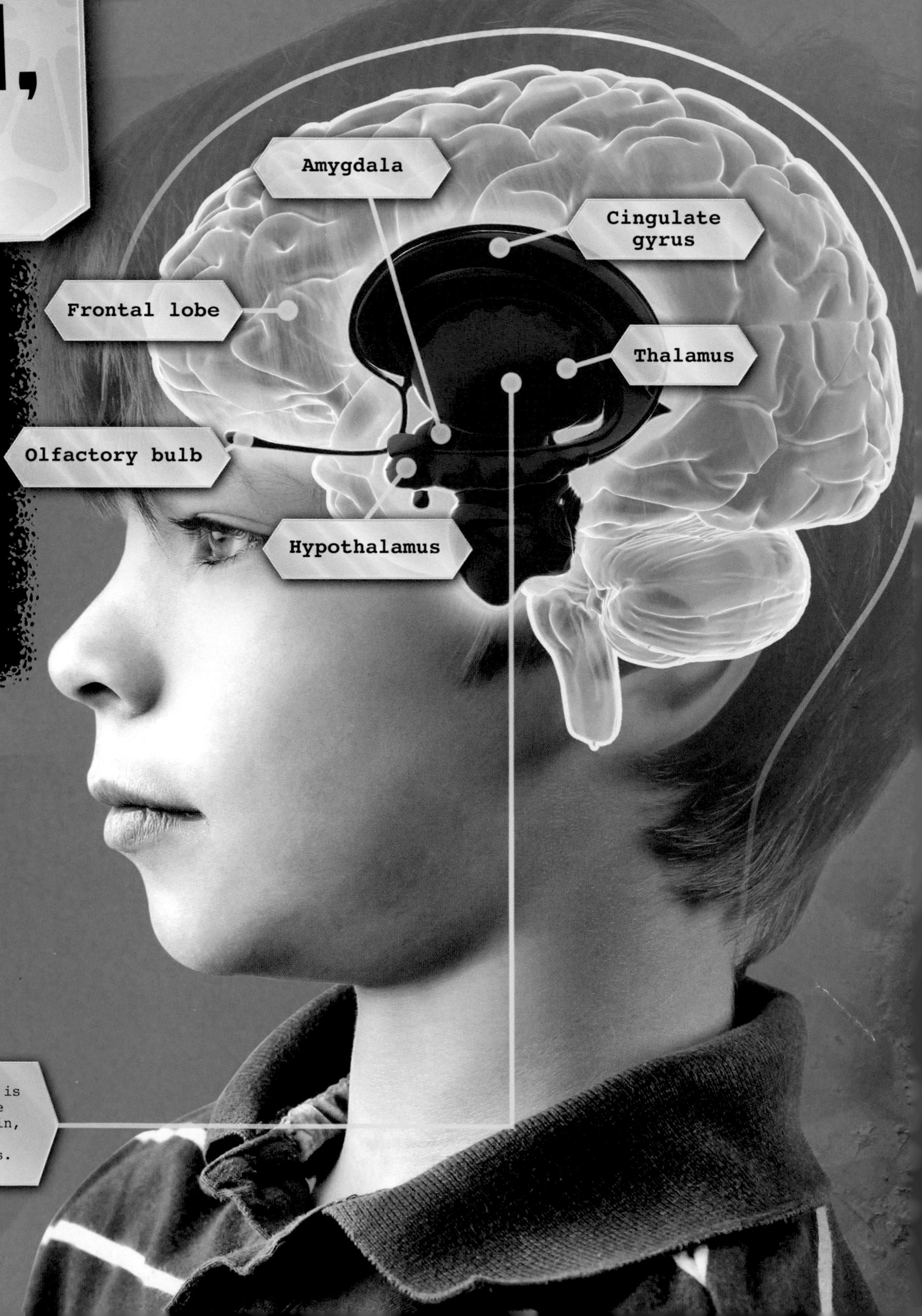

Amygdala

Cingulate gyrus

Frontal lobe

Thalamus

Olfactory bulb

Hypothalamus

Your limbic system is located deep in the centre of your brain, around a structure called the thalamus.

HAPPINESS

When you are happy, your brain is buzzing with neurotransmitters called serotonin and dopamine – your body's own feel-good chemicals. Interestingly, eating chocolate stimulates the brain to release serotonin and dopamine, too – and it even contains a compound called tryptophan, which the body uses to make more serotonin!

LOVE

A chemical compound called oxytocin is sometimes called the love hormone. It is released by the hypothalamus and also by a part of the brain called the pituitary gland. A mother's body produces lots of oxytocin during and after childbirth, and when she is breastfeeding her baby – and it seems to reinforce the bond between mother and child. And everyone's body produces lots of oxytocin when they feel love.

FEELING GOOD!

When you exercise, your nervous system produces chemical compounds called endorphins. The main job of endorphins is to reduce the sensation of pain, by damping down the activity of neurons involved in this feeling – but they also have an effect on the brain itself, where they generate feelings of euphoria (joy). So that's why you feel so good after playing!

THE BRAIN ACTIVATION PAGE

Watch your brain react as you experience different feelings!

FEAR

It is natural to be scared of some things – it can be essential to our survival – so some fears are natural reactions that we are born with. The amygdala is the main part of the brain involved in processing fear (and sadness, too). But we also learn to be scared of certain things, and the amygdala is a key part of that; it communicates with the hippocampus, which is the part of the brain that prepares memories for storage, and helps to retrieve them.

DISGUST

When you feel disgusted about something, your nose crumples up and you turn or pull away from whatever is upsetting you. The part of the limbic system most involved in the emotion of disgust is the olfactory bulb, which carries signals from the nose.

STRESSING AND RELAXING

You may have heard people saying they are really stressed – by work, or worries about an exam, for example. Stress is the body's natural way of dealing with threats to survival. Some of stress can improve your performance in tasks that require quick thinking, but too much is seriously bad for your health. So make sure you don't let stress take over – and find time to relax.

Hypothalamus

DANGER!

When your brain detects a threat, it sets off a chain of events that prepares your body for 'fight or flight', getting you ready to face up to the threat or make a hasty exit. It increases your heart and breathing rate, it diverts blood away from your digestive system so that more can flow to your muscles and your brain, and it heightens your senses.

> When you are in a scary situation your body feels 'on edge', and your brain is working hard and fast to find a quick way out or to face the threat head on.

CHEMICAL RELEASE

Your brain's reaction to a threat or a worry begins in the limbic system (see p. 20), the brain's emotional centre. Part of the limbic system, the hypothalamus, starts a chain of events that ends with the release of three 'stress hormones' into your bloodstream. These hormones – cortisol, adrenaline and noadrenaline – travel around the body, triggering the changes necessary to make your body ready to face the stressful situation.

Adrenal glands

Kidneys

The hypothalamus activates the pituitary gland, which releases a hormone called cortisol into your bloodstream. When cortisol reaches your kidneys, it activates another gland, called the adrenal gland. When cortisol reaches the brain, it causes the hypothalamus to stop the stress reaction — unless the threat or worry has not gone away.

DRY MOUTH, SWEATY PALMS

The hormones your adrenal gland releases when you are under stress affect nerves all over your body. These nerves can change the behaviour of organs: they stop your intestines digesting food; they widen the airways in your lungs; they send more blood to your brain. They also reduce the production of saliva in your mouth, cause your pupils to dilate (get bigger) and your skin to sweat.

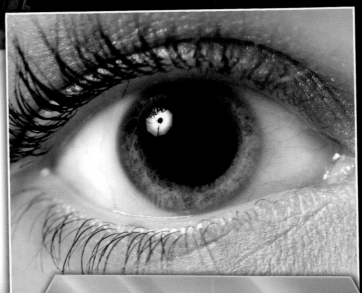

The pupil is a hole in the middle of the iris — the coloured part of the eye. The iris has muscles inside; under stressful conditions, nerves affected by stress hormones cause one set of muscles to contract, and the pupil widens to let in more light.

...AND RELAX!

After 'fight or flight' comes 'rest and digest'. When a stressful situation is over, your heart rate and breathing slow, digestion begins again, your pupils shrink, and your muscles relax. But if a worry continues, then cortisol levels remain high over long periods of time, and that can cause a range of health problems, from heart issues to obesity.

Once a threat or worry has gone away, the cortisol hormone, circulating in the bloodstream, makes the hypothalamus stop the stress response — and everything can go back to normal.

CLEVER BRAIN

Your brain keeps you alive and lets you perceive the world around you. Luckily for you, it also lets you do even more amazing things – things that make you really intelligent – for example, it can solve difficult problems, have an argument and plan your next move in a game of chess. Your brain can even help you wonder about how it works! All these abilities depend upon the outermost part of your brain: the cortex.

Accumbens

Frontal lobe

GREY MATTER

Thinking mostly happens in the cerebrum, the largest part of the brain – the part that looks like a walnut. It is the outermost part that works the hardest: the cortex (a Latin word meaning 'bark'). The cortex is made of 'grey matter', while the rest of the cerebrum is made of 'white matter'. Grey matter contains the cell bodies of billions of neurons, while the white matter is a tangle of axons and dendrites, the fibres that connect the neurons (see p. 8).

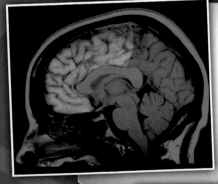

UP FRONT

The cerebral cortex has many specialized areas that are involved in particular tasks. For example, there are areas devoted to the senses – information from your eyes is processed in large regions at the back, and touch sensations from your body are processed in the temporal lobes. Most of the 'thinking' – decision-making, planning and problem-solving – takes place in the frontal lobes, just behind your forehead.

This picture is from a 3D MRI scan of a brain. The pink area in the frontal cortex shows which parts of the brain were working hardest when a person was thinking about words, before saying them.

FUN FACT!

More than 90% of the oxygen supplied to the brain goes to the grey matter.

When this guitarist is playing his solo, he has to listen to the rest of the band, think about what notes will work, all make his fingers move in the right way. It means most of his cerebral cortex is working really hard.

CREATIVE NOISE

Intelligence is much more than just being 'clever'. Some people are really creative, while some people are good at reading other people's emotions, for example. These are all forms of intelligence. Improvising – making up music as you go along – is a complex creative task, and scientists have shown it involves many parts of the cortex working together, including the auditory cortex (hearing), the visual cortex (sight), the sensory cortex (touching the instrument) and the frontal lobes (for planning).

JUST SAY NO

Have you ever really wanted something but had to wait before you could get it? It's called 'delayed gratification', and it's a skill that involves the cortex of the frontal lobes. Another area of the brain crucial in delayed gratification is the nucleus accumbens, which normally deals with pleasure and motivation – and there are very strong connections between these two areas.

Waiting for delayed gratification isn't always easy!

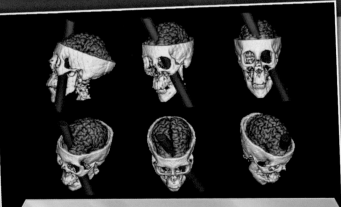

This picture shows the damage a metal rod caused when it went through Phineas Gage's skull in 1848, obliterating his frontal cortex. Before the accident he was a friendly and well-liked man, but without one of his frontal lobes his personality changed. Gage lived on for years, but acted as though he was a different person.

SOCIAL BRAIN

Human beings are social, which means they can get along with each other, become friends and share things. Social behaviour requires a lot of brainpower, and much of it happens in part of the frontal lobes called the prefrontal cortex. People who have damage to their prefrontal cortex find it hard to cope in groups of people, and they may lose the ability to be kind and considerate of others.

MIND YOUR LANGUAGE

All animals communicate, but no other species does it to the extent humans do. The power and richness of language – written and spoken – enable us to learn from each other, to express our thoughts, to argue and, sometimes, to get what we want. Speaking, listening, writing and reading involve lots of different parts of the brain, but there are particular areas of the cerebral cortex (see pp. 24–25) that have special functions.

Wernicke's area

Broca's area

WHERE IN THE BRAIN?

As you might expect for such a difficult task, the parts of the brain most heavily involved in speech are in the cortex (see pp. 24–25). Scientists know little about how the brain actually processes language – but from studying people with small areas damaged through injury or disease, they do know about two regions in the cortex that are crucial: Broca's area and Wernicke's area.

AMAZING BRAIN

When you think about it, language is incredibly complex: there are millions of words, and an infinite way of putting them together to form sentences. Many words sound or look the same but mean different things – and there are often many words for the same thing! On top of all that, when the brain is listening to speech, it has to cope with the different ways people speak, such as accents and speaking quickly or slowly.

!!!

!

:O

THE BRAIN ACTIVATION PAGE

Watch your brain react as it tries to predict what's going to happen next!

Your brain is able to listen to just the sound of one person's voice, and follow what they are saying to you, even in a noisy, crowded room.

SIGN LANGUAGE

People who are deaf often use sign language to communicate. Sign languages have all the same rules of grammar (sentence construction) and just as wide a vocabulary as spoken languages. It is no surprise, then, that people communicating by signing use the same parts of the brain as people speaking and listening.

EARLY ALPHABETS

The earliest written languages used pictograms: small, simple pictures that represented an idea or a thing. Stringing these together, people in early civilizations could tell stories and write things down. Gradually, people began to use a small set of pictograms to represent sounds instead – the first alphabet.

The first alphabet was made up of 24 Egyptian hieroglyphics. Each symbol stood for a particular sound. All modern written languages use symbols to represent sounds, which make it easy to learn a language — but once you have learned to read, the brain can recognize whole words at a time.

SURPRISE YOUR BRAIN

One of the most important jobs of your intelligent brain is to predict what happens next. That's really important in reading or hearing sentences: you almost always predict how a sentence will ... end. Your brain is constantly working out what is most likely to happen, based on what it has experienced before. So when something is not as expected, the brain really takes notice. If a sentence ends in a surprising way – it might be a joke or a nonsense word, for example – your brain responds with a rapid wave of electricity, which sweeps across the whole cortex.

When lots of the brain's neurons fire at once — for example, when you hear a surprising word — they produce an electrical signal that can be detected by placing electrodes on the skin around the head.

REMEMBERING AND FORGETTING

One of the most important things your brain does is to make and retrieve memories. It helps you learn to recognize faces and other objects, it helps you to become aware of dangers and pleasures, and it helps you make sense of your life. Your brain's memories are held in various parts of the cortex (see pp. 24–25), but other brain structures are involved in storing and retrieving them, and in deciding which memories you need to hold on to.

MAKING MEMORIES

Memories are 'encoded' into synapses – the tiny gaps at the points where neurons meet (see p. 9). Each synapse will either encourage, or 'excite', a neuron to fire or discourage, or 'stop' it. New sensations, experiences and thoughts affect the amount by which the synapses do this – and, remarkably, that is how memories are stored.

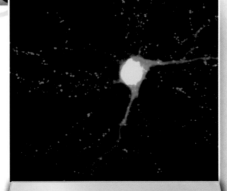

In this picture, scientists used fluorescent (glowing) chemicals to light up the synapses around a single neuron taken from a mouse. Each green dot is a synapse that excites the main neuron, while the red dots are synapses that inhibit it. Mouse memory — and human memory — is held in these patterns of synapses.

THE BRAIN
ACTIVATION PAGE

Test your memory to activate your cortex!

SHORT-TERM MEMORY

Short-term memory, held in the prefrontal cortex (see pp. 24–25), is temporary, and is quickly replaced by new things. You use it for things like remembering the beginning of this sentence while you read all the way to the full stop. Research shows that people can usually only hold around five separate things in their short-term memory before it becomes 'full'.

We use short-term memory when we are trying to find something; and sometimes when we enter a room the memory of what we are looking for has disappeared!

Your brain remembers special occasions, such as birthday parties, because they are pleasurable and you are surrounded by people who mean a lot to you.

LONG-TERM MEMORY

Long-term memory has an endless capacity for storing information and experiences, and it can hold on to these memories for a lifetime. Scientists have discovered that the amygdala and the hippocampus (see pp. 20–21) are heavily involved in deciding which memories to commit to long-term storage. These structures are part of the limbic system, which deals with emotion – so we are most likely to remember things that are scary or pleasurable, things that have emotional meaning.

Some people who have trained to make their memory really good compete in memory championships, where they may have to remember the order of packs of playing cards or very long lists of random numbers or words.

MEMORY FEATS

People can train their memories to recall huge amounts of information. Most people do it by making the information into stories. So, for example, to remember a list of random words, you can build the words into a story, which you can also visualize, a bit like watching a film in your mind. However strange the story may seem, it will help you to remember the list of words. Why not try it? It works for remembering song lyrics, too.

During a single night's sleep, the brain goes through various stages. Each stage has a different pattern of brain waves — electrical activity across all the brain's neurons. The brain seems to consolidate long-term memories during slow-wave, or delta, sleep.

MEMORY AND SLEEP

Research has shown that sleep is essential in consolidating memories; this means storing away memories you have made during the day, in a form that the brain can access later. This is why your dreams often involve versions of events that have happened during the day. People who do not get enough sleep can have real problems with their memories.

SOUTH PARK TOWNSHIP LIBRARY

29

UTHER BRAINS

The human brain is truly remarkable, but how does it compare to the brains of other animals? Some animals have brains that are much bigger than ours – although most are smaller. Some animals have no brains at all – just simple networks of neurons. As far as we know, no other animals are as intelligent as we are – but one day, computers might be!

BIGGER THAN YOUR BRAIN

All mammals have brains that are similar to yours, with a cerebrum, a cerebral cortex and a spinal cord. Some mammals have brains bigger than a fully developed human brain. For example, an adult elephant's brain has a mass of about 4.8 kilograms and an adult sperm whale's brain has a mass of about 8 kilograms – compared with about 1.4 kilograms for an adult human.

Human

Bear

BIRD BRAIN

The term 'bird brain' is often used to suggest someone has little intelligence. Birds do have small brains, and they lack the cerebral cortex that gives us humans some of our most intelligent qualities – but many birds are surprisingly intelligent. The most intelligent kinds of birds are in the group *Corvus*, which includes crows, jackdaws, jays, ravens and magpies.

This crow has worked out that it can drink if it uses stones to raise the water level in this beaker.